I0051867

Women's Leadership Handbook

Copyright © 2021 by Susan K. Wehrley

All rights reserved. No part of this book may be used or reproduced in any manner whatsoever without the written permission of the author, Susan K. Wehrley, except in the case of brief quotations embodied in critical articles or reviews. All photos used with permission and/or credit given.

Published by Thomas & Kay Publishing

Printed by Create Space in the United States of American

10 9 8 7 6 5 4 3 2 1

Library of Congress Cataloging-in Publication Data is available for this title.

ISBN: 978-0-9729505-7-2

Contact:
Email: Susan@BIZremedies.com
Websites: www.BIZremedies.com &
www.TheAlignAcademy.com where you will find the
Cheetah School for Women Leaders

From the Author

I have always loved Cheetahs. Some say perhaps they are my Spirit Animal. Honestly, I didn't even know there was such a thing—nor do I know if I really believe in that or not.

But, when I read about the Cheetah, I resonated with everything about them! What do I love about the cheetah? They are **fearless** and **focused**—seizing the opportunities to go after exactly what they want with right action. In addition, they are **fabulous** and know how to pivot when needed, because they are the fastest land animal in the world. As a result, they can prioritize and achieve their goals!

You too can be like the cheetah—*fearless, focused, and fabulous*! Because I am committed to helping you create the life you want, I have taken some of the most popular skills from my online program called, *Cheetah School for Women Leaders*—and put it into this easy-to-use Women's Leadership Handbook.

Once you've completed this book, go deeper in your learning by joining my online *Cheetah School for Women Leaders*—where you will find on-demand videos and training to help you create the life you love at: www.TheAlignAcademy.com . Redeem this coupon code and receive $50 off your enrollment: IBoughtTheWomensLeadershipHandbook2021

Wishing you life's best-
Susan

Preface:
Why Cheetah?

The McKinsey Study tells us that women leaders out rank men in 17 out of 19 leadership characteristics. But where women need to improve is: Negotiation and Risk-taking.

That's why we can learn a lot from the cheetah who is fearless, focused and fabulous!

The spirit of the cheetah teaches us to:

- **AWAKEN** to what you want. As your desire expands, you will become *fearless.*

- **GOAL-ALIGNMENT** so you can be *focused* and align your decisions to your vision, values, and goals!

- **PIVOT** when things don't align to what you want, you will make the changes needed to succeed because you not only know you are enough—you know you are *fabulous* and therefore 'this or something better' is on its way!

When we develop the spirit of the cheetah, we awaken to what we want; align our decisions to our vision, values and goals and pivot to stay in alignment. This means we take the risks we need to succeed and unapologetically negotiate on our behalf; instead of always playing it nice. When we make this shift in our approach, we become effective leaders, at work and home.

Chapters

AWAKEN:
Be Fearless!

AWAKEN:
Your Wisdom & Guts!

In order to create the life you love, you need to awaken to your wisdom, as well as have the guts to do something about what you know. When you awaken to your wisdom & guts, you will be like the cheetah—fearless! This means you will take the risks you need to succeed and negotiate on your behalf when necessary. Yes, it takes wisdom & guts to claim what you want in the following 7 areas of your life:

- Financially

- Physically

- Emotionally

- Mentally

- Spiritually

- Relationally

- Vocationally

It takes wisdom & guts to make effective decisions that align to your vision, values, and goals!

Wisdom means making decisions that are right for you—because it's all about awakening to your vision, values and goals, and aligning your decisions accordingly. To have guts means you are fearless and focused on what you want; instead of how others might react.

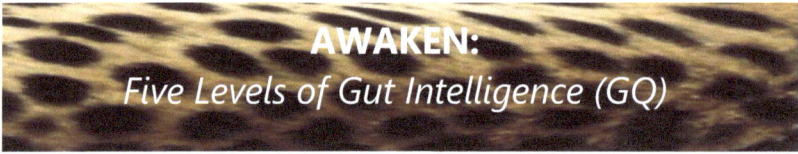

Fear occurs when we are not intuitively aligned to our inner voice and inner authority. This inner voice and inner authority is our Gut Intelligence (GQ):

Gut Intelligence (GQ) is:
The Wisdom to know the truth and the guts to do something about it.

Gut Intelligence (GQ) is like having the animal instinct of the cheetah. It is an ability to get beyond fear and detach from what other's think and expect from us so we can hear our inner voice guide us. It is best explained if I share with you the 5 Levels of Gut Intelligence, so you can see how this transformation from outer authority to inner authority works.

5 Levels of Gut Intelligence (GQ):
Level One: Unconsciousness
Level Two: Judgment & Self-Doubt
Level Three: Self-Awareness
Level Four: Detachment
Level Five: Intuitive Alignment

Level One: Unconsciousness:

We create unconsciousness by addictions and distractions. Addictions can be anything from:

- Drinking

- Drugs

- Over-eating

- Gambling

- Over-spending

...Anything that distracts you and keeps you from listening within to that gut-alert will put you in a state of unconsciousness. Distractions may be a need to stay busy, so you don't have to be conscious of what is going on around you or within you.

That's why we use addictions and distractions—so we don't have to deal with reality and our fear.

JOURNAL: What gut-alert are you not dealing with? What is your addiction or distraction of choice?

Level Two: Judgment & Self-Doubt:

At this level we begin to feel our fear! Think of an animal, like the cheetah, that has a warning signal that says, "Stay away from this! This is dangerous!" They don't cognitively process this fear in their head. They just trust their instincts. Our Gut Intelligence (GQ) is our instinct that says, "Pay attention!"

At this level you have a choice: To slip back to level one unconsciousness, or to move forward and become more self-aware of the fear. Moving forward allows you to deal with the judgment and the self-doubt that is holding you back from listening to your inner authority.

JOURNAL: What judgment and self-doubt is holding you back? Is the judgment towards yourself or others?

Level Three: Self-Awareness

This level can bring up a lot of emotions in addition to fear and self-doubt. Working with the emotions will help you to get to the next level of consciousness, which is detachment. But first, you need to understand how to work with the emotions to awaken to greater consciousness, so you can stop reacting in a fight or flight manner. Here are 4 common emotions that cause us to react:

- *Anger:* Is simply an emotion that tells us: "I don't like this! I want it to change!" We need to ask our self, "What needs to change?" There is wisdom in that conversation with our self!

- *Shame:* A feeling of being less than or not enough.

- *Sadness:* Tells us we believe we lost something. What is it? Why was it important to us? These are answers we need to understand to move forward so we can let go and learn what we want.

- *Fear:* Is an emotion that tells us we are afraid we cannot handle something. When you ask yourself, "How might I handle that?" and listen to your inner voice, you get past your fear.

JOURNAL: What emotions and reactions are you becoming aware of?

Level Four: Detachment:

When we finally understand our emotions—we can let them guide us and then let go of them! This allows us to take those emotions into consideration, without letting them drive us to an impulsive fight or flight reaction!

To help us detach, we can ask our self these two questions?

- What are my emotions trying to tell me?

- What do I need to detach from so I can make a wise decision?

When we ask our self these questions, we detach from the emotion and create a space for wisdom to speak to us.

JOURNAL: What do you need to detach from?

Level Five: Intuitive Alignment:

To allow intuition to guide you, you need to quiet the mind through deep breathing. Only then can you stop the chattering mind of your ego and create a space for intuition in your life.

Intuition will not come barging in. It must be invited. We sometimes don't invite intuition in because we are afraid of knowing; or afraid of letting go of control. That's why we must pass through level 4: Detachment, first. Then, we can quiet our chattering mind and ask our intuition, *"How might I make a decision that aligns to my vision, values and goals?"*

JOURNAL: Where in your life are you ready to detach and invite intuition in to guide you?

AWAKEN:
Your Three Brains

To achieve wisdom and higher levels of intuitive alignment, we need to consider our 3 brains:

- **Gut:** Alert us to what we need to notice.

- **Heart:** Aligns us to what we value, so that we can make decisions based on what matters most to us.

- **Head:** Assimilates the possibilities to give us the best decision for us.

Just like the cheetah, when our 3 brains work well together, it is like an effective Board of Directors within. When they don't work well together, we:

- Are in a state of confusion.

- Feel fear and anxiety about the unknown.

- Feel a bit depressed because we don't have the guts to do what our intuition is guiding us to do.

JOURNAL: Have you been feeling confused, anxious, or depressed?

AWAKEN:
The Role of the Gut

We do not want to make decisions on the gut alone. Our gut's function is to simply alert us: "Something's going on here!" If we make a quick decision without synchronizing the heart and the head, our gut will send a message to the amygdala part of our brain—which is the fight or flight reaction center.

The awaken the gut, spend time:

- Wondering

- Being curious

- Asking it questions

This will help you understand what the gut-alert is trying to tell you. Once you feel clear, then you're ready to awaken your heart, so you can understand more of its function.

As you awaken each one of your brains, you will increase your Gut Intelligence (GQ).

JOURNAL: What's one thing your gut has been trying to tell you?

AWAKEN:
The Role of the Heart

Being able to understand emotions, helps us to get beyond our fear and awaken the role of the heart. For example:

- *Sadness* means we feel like we have lost something.

- *Anger* tells us something has to change.

- *Overwhelmed* makes us feel out of control.

- *Disappointment* tells us something did not meet our expectations.

- *Fear* makes us believe we aren't enough to get what we want.

Use these 3 steps to awaken your heart:

1. **Identify** your emotions—name them.

2. **Explore** the wisdom of emotions—what are they telling you?

3. **Discover** how your emotions are aligning you to what you want.

JOURNAL: How are your emotions aligning you to what you want?

AWAKEN:
The Role of the Head

To awaken to the role of the head, which is to find the best possibilities for our situation, we need to do two things:

#1: Gain knowledge and learn

#2: Engage your mind with this question: *"How might I make a decision that aligns with my vision, values and goals?"*

JOURNAL:

- Think of a situation you want to improve. Where can you gain knowledge and learn more about possibilities?

- What possibilities are you already thinking about?

Remember:
-*Your gut's function is to alert you* to pay attention!
-*Your heart's function is to align you* to what you want!
-*Your head's function is to assimilate the* information to find the best possibility for you!

To integrate your gut, heart and head in decision-making, ask the following questions:

JOURNAL:

- **GUT QUESTION:** What is my gut alerting me to notice?

- **HEART QUESTION:** What are my emotions telling me I value in this situation?

- **HEAD QUESTION:** What possibilities exist to get what I want?

AWAKEN:
Affirmations for the Gut, Heart & Head

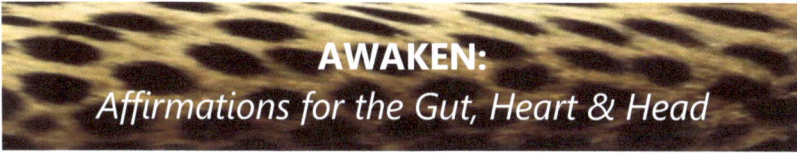

Gut Affirmations

- I AM able to trust my gut-alert

- I AM able to notice cues at the tip of the iceberg

- I AM able to notice if something is not congruent

- I AM able to listen, beyond words, to the tone of voice, body language and emotional energy

Heart Affirmations:

- I AM able to identify my emotions

- I AM able to be curious about what they're telling me

- I AM able to understand the wisdom of my emotions and how they align me to what I value

- I AM able to honor myself and what I value

Head Affirmations:

- I AM able to pause, and take a deep breath, so I AM able to make the very best choice for me!

- I AM able to resist the impulsivity of a fight or fight reaction

- I AM able to hear my Intuitive Inner Voice

- I AM able to breathe deeply to quiet my mind so I know exactly what I need to do or say in the moment that matters!

AWAKEN:
8 Wellness Practices

Wellness not only increases Gut Intelligence (GQ), it gives you more wisdom in decision-making. When we take care of our gut health—we're able to be more fearless, focused & fabulous—like the cheetah!

Our gut is not just a brain for decision-making; our gut is our immune system as well. So, we want to be sure we're practicing these 8 wellness practices:

For the Mind:

Wellness Practice #1: Sleep

A lot people don't understand how important it is to sleep. And how much sleep is enough! Most people need 7-8 hours of sleep every day. But the problem is: If they're not stopping to listen to their gut-alert—they often will not be able to sleep. If we don't get a solid 7-8 hours of sleep, we will have a difficult time being fearless, focused and feeling fabulous throughout the day!

JOURNAL: Do you need to do a better job at stopping to listen to your gut-alert throughout the day?

Wellness Practice #2: Thoughts and Journaling

One of the ways that we can pay attention to our gut-alert throughout the day is to journal. When you journal, stop and think about these 4 questions:

JOURNAL: When you get a gut-alert, think about these 4 questions:

- What was my *gut-alert* trying to tell me?

- How is my *heart aligning* me to what I want?

- What possibilities is my *head assimilating*?

- How is my *intuition* trying to guide me?

Journaling throughout the day on these 4 questions can help you become fearless, focused, and fabulous once again!

Wellness Practice #3: Breathing and Meditation for Clarity

When we use the S.T.O.P. Technique throughout the day, we gain more clarity. Breathing deeply into our gut, improves the gut-brain axis and our ability to awaken to higher levels of consciousness. Practice these 4 steps below to the S.T.O.P. Technique throughout the day when you get a gut alert. It will help you quiet your mind so you can hear your intuition within.

S.T.O.P. Technique:
S-slow down and breathe
T-tune in within
O-observe what is happening
P-perceive a new possibility

JOURNAL: Flush out the S.T.O.P. Technique for one of your situations, after you slow down and breathe:

What did you notice when you tuned in?

What did you observe?

What possibilities are you realizing?

For the Heart:

Wellness Practice #4: Emotional Management

What does Emotional Management mean? It means to be curious about what your emotions are trying to tell you. Once you put words to your emotions, you are in control of your emotions—instead of your emotions being in control of you. Literally, you are moving from the emotional center of your brain to the executive center of your brain when you become curious about your emotions. Emotional management occurs when you take the time to be curious and understand what your emotions are trying to tell you.

JOURNAL: For practice: Journal about one emotion you are experiencing. Get curious about it:

Wellness Practice #5: Gratitude and Surrender

Start every day with a cup that is half-full at least.

To start the day, say:

- I'm happy to be alive!

- I'm happy that today I'm healthy

- I'm happy that my body is serving me today

- I'm happy that I'm safe today

- I'm happy that I have enough food for today

- I'm happy that I have enough money to have the lights on today and to have a roof over my head today

- I'm happy that I have something that I'm doing that I love today

JOURNAL: Make a list of what you are grateful for:

For the Gut:

Wellness Practice #6: Food & Hydration

Food and hydration are an important part of wellness. First, water is very important. But not all water is the same. Often, tap water has too much chlorine in it for our gut. Drinking purified water is important; or glass bottled water. Plastic bottled water—not so good! Because that plastic can really change the hormones in our gut.

And it's important to have about 8 glasses of water a day. So, continue to hydrate yourself: 2 glasses in the morning, couple at noon, a few in the afternoon, and a couple at night. It is important to hydrate yourself throughout the whole day.

Not all food is the same either. We want to stay away from things like:

- Sugar

- Processed food

We want to be eating more things like:

- Whole grains

- Freshly made sauerkraut

- Black Tea

- Kombucha Tea

- Oranges

- Vegetables: Artichokes, Lentils, Onions, Soybeans, Leaks, Asparagus

- Grass fed butter

- Dark Chocolate (if you want dessert)

- Cultured Yogurt

- Spices

- Garlic

Foods to avoid:

- Antibiotics

- Fried foods

- Red meat

- Processed and packaged junk food

- Food high in sugar

- Limited refined carbs

- Dairy products

- Refined oil

- Baked goods

JOURNAL: How might you adjust your food & water intake?

Wellness Practice #7: Movement

Another wellness practice is movement. I don't want to use the word, "Exercise". I want to use the word, "Movement", because our body retains our emotions and there's a saying that says, "Your issues our in your tissues." That's why yoga has become popular. When we do yoga, we're burning the muscles in certain areas, as we're breathing deeply into our body and releasing those emotions—those issues in our tissues.

But you don't have to do Yoga. I talk to people who are runners, and they say that's their form of yoga. This can be true for cyclers or someone who walks briskly. When you're moving your body and breathing deeply, you are using movement for overall wellness. So, while I like yoga as a practice of movement, I think any kind of movement is great! Even vigorous house cleaning can be great for us because when we move and breathe deeply—we're moving the issues in our tissues.

JOURNAL: What kind of movement helps you to breathe deeply so you can move the issues in your tissues?

Wellness Practice #8: Ground yourself in nature

There's something about nature that makes us breathe more deeply. Nature brings us back to our essence and gets us out of our head, so we can be fearless, focused & fabulous—like the cheetah!

Even though our head is a brain, and we give honor to it—often times we are way too much up in our head and not balanced enough in our body (our gut and heart). Nature brings us back into our body—and helps us to get in balance.

JOURNAL:
What aspects of nature brings you back in balance?

Now that you have learned about the 8 Wellness Practices, it's time to create a plan of action. Use the worksheet below to chart out your plan.

Wellness Action: Your Plan for these 8 Wellness Practices:

What   *When*

Mind:

#1: SLEEP:

#2: JOURNALING:

#3: MEDITATION:

Notes:

Heart:

#4: EMOTIONAL MANAGEMENT:

#5: GRATITUDE & SURRENDER:

Notes:

Gut:

#6: NUTRITION & HYDRATION:

#7: MOVEMENT:

#8: NATURE:

Notes:

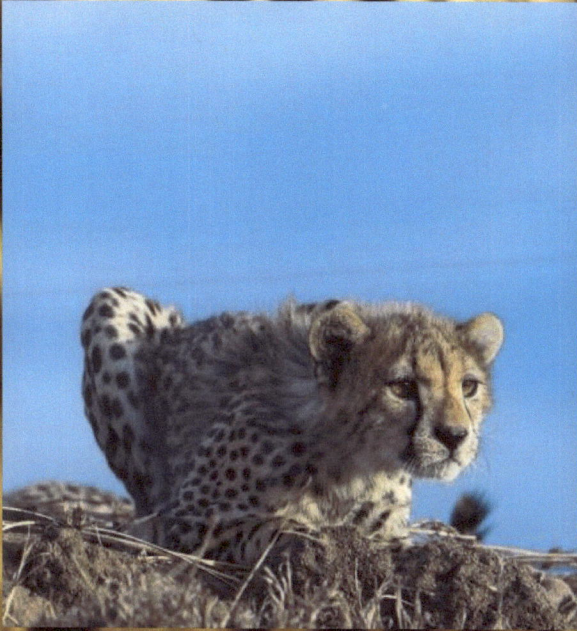

GOAL-ALIGNMENT:
Be Focused!

GOAL-ALIGNMENT:
Focus on your Vision, Values, and Goals!

When you create a vision, values, and goals for the 7 different faucets of your life, you become the cheetah—focused! It's important that we have our vision, values, and goals outlined because then, in the moment of choice, we can make effective decisions. We do this by using the S.T.O.P. Technique from the previous chapter and asking our self:

- What is my vision?

- What are my values?

- What are my goals?

- How might I align my decisions accordingly?

This helps us to raise our level of consciousness and choose the life we love!

JOURNAL: Name a time you did this recently? Did you feel more fearless, focused & fabulous like the cheetah?

GOAL-ALIGNMENT:
Create from your Essence

Stopping and aligning your decision to your vision, values, and goals become easier when you chart them out clearly. In order to do this, let's first make sure they are authentic to you!

Often, we have this voice chattering in our head, that tells us:

- "We should be doing this!"

- "We should be doing that!"

- "This is what's best for us!"

This is the voice of our ego that was developed and conditioned by:

- Society

- Mom, Dad or some kind of authority figure in your life

Our ego tries to help us fit in so we can feel safe, secure, loved and belonging to a group. We learn to believe fitting in will make us safe and happy! This, however, is not true. What makes us safe and happy is when we listen to that voice of inner authority—our intuition, which I also refer to as "Gut Intelligence" (GQ).

We know we are listening to our intuition when we integrate the wisdom from our three brains:

1. It has to make sense in your **HEAD**, so you can be *fearless* enough to imagine it occurring.

2. You have to feel the desire in your **HEART**, so you can stay *focused* on it.

3. You have to know it in your **GUT** you are *fabulous* enough to make it happen!

JOURNAL: Think about something you want and do a check-in:

- **HEAD-check**: Do you feel *fearless* enough that you can imagine it happening the way you want it to?

- **HEART-check**: Do you desire it enough to want to be *focused* on it?

- **GUT-check**: Do you think you are *fabulous* enough to get it (or this or something better)?

Doing this check-in, allows you to notice if you have any incongruencies between the gut, heart, and head. When they all agree—your chance of manifesting what you say you want is much greater!

GOAL-ALIGNMENT:
Change your "but" to "and"

Often when our gut, heart, and head do not agree. We might say we want one thing, but unconsciously we fear we might have to give up something else to get it. This is called, "limited-thinking". For example, we might think:

- I want the love of my life, **but I'm afraid** there aren't any good men (or women) out there

- Or, I really want to make more money, **but I don't want to be focused** on work and give up all my free time

- Or, I really want to have this business, **but I don't think I'm fabulous** enough to be successful

- When we change our **"but" to "and"**, we begin to realize the possibilities that exist for us to have everything we want. For example, we would change the first sentence like this: I want the love of my life, **and I'm sure** there are many good men (or women) out there

JOURNAL: Now, take a sentence above and change your "but" to "and". Or make up one of your own.

GOAL-ALIGNMENT:
The Magic of "How might I....?"

Often, subconsciously, we tell ourselves, "I'm not fabulous enough to get what I want!" This may sound like:

- "I'm not enough to have the work life I want and the love life I want!"

- "I'm not enough to be successful!"

When we focus on the question,

"How might I...?",

we open our mindset and allow intuition to guide us to what we want and how we can get it. Where do you need to create a *"How might I...?"* question?"

JOURNAL: What is your *"How might I...?"* question

GOAL-ALIGNMENT:
Your Vision & Your "WHY"

Now that we have cleared out your ego a bit and opened your mind to, "how might you create the life you want?", let's focus on creating a vision. A vision statement is your "WHY" you do what you do. It's what gives purpose or meaning behind your life, at work and at home. It mirrors your essence.

A vision is a one-word sentence that begins with, "To...(something)"

For example, when you look at Walt Disney's amusement parks—their vision isn't to sell tickets to all amusement parks. That's what they do. Their vision is to create happy memories. That's the "WHY" behind what they do.

JOURNAL:

When you are without fear, what do you want to create more than anything else?

"To...

How to Create a Vision Board

A vision board helps you figure out your vision. It takes the unconscious knowing of your mind and brings it into consciousness.

Here are the steps to create a vision board:

1. **Buy magazines**-that represent what you like, from professional to personal. So, go to Walgreens or Barnes and Noble and pick off magazines on the shelf if you don't have them. Then, page through those magazines. Don't consciously go out to seek to find something.

2. **See what gets your attention**. Could be pictures or words. Anything that makes you go, "Awww 😊". Anything that magnetizes you towards those words or pictures. Or gives you a "feel good" feeling. Rip it out of the magazine!

3. **Make a pile** of those things that caught your attention in a positive sort of way.

4. **Get poster board.**

5. **Scissors and a glue stick**. You don't have to use a scissors. You can have raged edges, that's fine. But most people like to cut out their words and pictures. So, as you go through the pile, and you're cutting out each one, ask yourself, "Does this still make me feel good?" If so, keep it.

6. **Place on vision board.** You don't have to organize it in a linear sort of way—with personal and professional in certain corners.

Note, that it's important to do the exercise with a very open and curious mindset. As you are paging through the magazine, ask yourself, "What feels good?" If it feels good, rip it out of the magazine. Same thing when you go to paste up on your poster board. Ask yourself if it still feels good. If it does, ask yourself where it should go on your poster board. Notice the open mindset of curiosity, so you're letting Intuitive lead and guide you.

JOURNAL: Now that you have your poster board done, look at it with that same curious open mindset. Ask yourself, "Hmmm...what is this telling me about a vision for my life?"

How might you put this into a vision statement: "To..."

GOAL ALIGNMENT:
Your Values & What Matters Most!

Now that you have created your vision statement, it's time to create your values. Values are important to make decisions in alignment with the life you want to create. It's important to understand your values because, in those moments of choice, where you have to make a tough decision, you will know what decision is best for you. Values are guideposts for decision-making.

Your values can change, depending on what is going on in your life. Below are some examples of values in 3 different categories. Pick a total of 8-10 values from the suggestions below; or create your own:

1. **Physical Values**

- Accuracy

- Cleanliness

- Maximizing Utilization and Resources

- Punctuality and Timeliness

- Quality of (Work: Products of Service) or (Home: Living)

- Regularity

- Dependability

- Responsiveness

- Safety

- Speed of Operations

- Speed of Things

2. **Organizational Values**

- Accountability

- Communication

- Cooperation and Teamwork

- Coordination

- Discipline

- Freedom for Initiative

- Integration

- Standardization

- Systemization

3. **Psychological Values**

- Problem-solving

- Continuous Improvement

- Creativity

- Customer Delight (Family, couple, personal)

- Decisiveness

- Developing other people

- Harmony (Peace)

- Integrity

- Loyalty

- Trust

- Respect

- Service to Society

- Will to Succeed

- Positive Attitude

JOURNAL: List 8-10 values:

1._____

2._____

3._____

4._____

5._____

6._____

7._____

8._____

9._____

10._____

GOAL ALIGNMENT:
Create your Goals!

Now that you have your vision and values, it's time to create your goals. Below you will see the 7 areas of your life. You will create personal goals for each one of them below:

1. Vocational

2. Financial

3. Relational

4. Physical

5. Spiritual

6. Emotional

7. Mental

Below are 7 areas at work. Choose up to 5 areas to focus on:

- Profit

- Revenue

- Marketing

- Customer Service

- Operations

- Culture

- IT

On the next pages are worksheets to use to create your personal and work goals. Use one worksheet per goal so you can flush out the details.

PERSONAL GOAL WORKSHEET:

The 7 Areas of Your Life (Check off one area to work on below):

__Vocational
__Financial
__Relational
__Physical
__Mental
__Emotional
__Spiritual

What is your overall vision statement for this goal?:

To_____

_____.

Create a minimum of 3 Milestones to help you reach your goal with actionable steps under each milestone. Be sure to commit to a timeline.

Milestone #1:_____

action step: _____ timeline_____
action step: _____ timeline_____
action step: _____ timeline_____

Milestone #2:_____

action step: _____ timeline_____
action step: _____ timeline_____
action step: _____ timeline_____

Milestone #3:_____

action step: _____ timeline_____
action step: _____ timeline_____
action step: _____ timeline_____

PERSONAL GOAL WORKSHEET:

The 7 Areas of Your Life (Check off one area to work on below):
__Vocational
__Financial
__Relational
__Physical
__Mental
__Emotional
__Spiritual

What is your overall vision statement for this goal?:
To_____
_____.

Create a minimum of 3 Milestones to help you reach your goal with actionable steps under each milestone. Be sure to commit to a timeline.

Milestone #1:_____
action step: _____ timeline_____
action step: _____ timeline_____
action step: _____ timeline_____

Milestone #2:_____
action step: _____ timeline_____
action step: _____ timeline_____
action step: _____ timeline_____

Milestone #3:_____
action step: _____ timeline_____
action step: _____ timeline_____
action step: _____ timeline_____

PERSONAL GOAL WORKSHEET:

The 7 Areas of Your Life (Check off one area to work on below):
__Vocational
__Financial
__Relational
__Physical
__Mental
__Emotional
__Spiritual

What is your overall vision statement for this goal?:
To_____
_____.

Create a minimum of 3 Milestones to help you reach your goal with actionable steps under each milestone. Be sure to commit to a timeline.

Milestone #1:_____
action step: _____ timeline_____
action step: _____ timeline_____
action step: _____ timeline_____

Milestone #2:_____
action step: _____ timeline_____
action step: _____ timeline_____
action step: _____ timeline_____

Milestone #3:_____
action step: _____ timeline_____
action step: _____ timeline_____
action step: _____ timeline_____

PERSONAL GOAL WORKSHEET:

The 7 Areas of Your Life (Check off one area to work on below):
__Vocational
__Financial
__Relational
__Physical
__Mental
__Emotional
__Spiritual

What is your overall vision statement for this goal?:
To_____
_____.

Create a minimum of 3 Milestones to help you reach your goal with actionable steps under each milestone. Be sure to commit to a timeline.

Milestone #1:_____
action step: _____ timeline_____
action step: _____ timeline_____
action step: _____ timeline_____

Milestone #2:_____
action step: _____ timeline_____
action step: _____ timeline_____
action step: _____ timeline_____

Milestone #3:_____
action step: _____ timeline_____
action step: _____ timeline_____
action step: _____ timeline_____

PERSONAL GOAL WORKSHEET:

The 7 Areas of Your Life (Check off one area to work on below):
__Vocational
__Financial
__Relational
__Physical
__Mental
__Emotional
__Spiritual

What is your overall vision statement for this goal?:
To_____
_____.

Create a minimum of 3 Milestones to help you reach your goal with actionable steps under each milestone. Be sure to commit to a timeline.

Milestone #1:_____
action step: _____ timeline_____
action step: _____ timeline_____
action step: _____ timeline_____

Milestone #2:_____
action step: _____ timeline_____
action step: _____ timeline_____
action step: _____ timeline_____

Milestone #3:_____
action step: _____ timeline_____
action step: _____ timeline_____
action step: _____ timeline_____

PERSONAL GOAL WORKSHEET:

The 7 Areas of Your Life (Check off one area to work on below):

_Vocational
_Financial
_Relational
_Physical
_Mental
_Emotional
_Spiritual

What is your overall vision statement for this goal?:

To_____

_____.

Create a minimum of 3 Milestones to help you reach your goal with actionable steps under each milestone. Be sure to commit to a timeline.

Milestone #1:_____

action step: _____   timeline_____
action step: _____   timeline_____
action step: _____   timeline_____

Milestone #2:_____

action step: _____   timeline_____
action step: _____   timeline_____
action step: _____   timeline_____

Milestone #3:_____

action step: _____   timeline_____
action step: _____   timeline_____
action step: _____   timeline_____

PERSONAL GOAL WORKSHEET:

The 7 Areas of Your Life (Check off one area to work on below):
__Vocational
__Financial
__Relational
__Physical
__Mental
__Emotional
__Spiritual

What is your overall vision statement for this goal?:
To_____
_____.

Create a minimum of 3 Milestones to help you reach your goal with actionable steps under each milestone. Be sure to commit to a timeline.

Milestone #1:_____
action step: _____ timeline_____
action step: _____ timeline_____
action step: _____ timeline_____

Milestone #2:_____
action step: _____ timeline_____
action step: _____ timeline_____
action step: _____ timeline_____

Milestone #3:_____
action step: _____ timeline_____
action step: _____ timeline_____
action step: _____ timeline_____

BUSINESS GOAL WORKSHEET:

The 7 Areas of Business Development (Choose only up to 5 goals):

___Profit
___Revenue
___Marketing
___Customer Service
___Operations
___Culture
___IT

What is your overall vision statement for the goal you chose?:
To_____
_____.

Name a minimum of 3 Milestones to help you reach your goal with actionable steps under each milestone. Be sure to commit to a timeline:

Milestone #1:_____
action step: _____ timeline_____
action step: _____ timeline_____
action step: _____ timeline_____

Milestone #2:_____
action step: _____ timeline_____
action step: _____ timeline_____
action step: _____ timeline_____

Milestone #3:_____
action step: _____ timeline_____
action step: _____ timeline_____
action step: _____ timeline_____

BUSINESS GOAL WORKSHEET:
The 7 Areas of Business Development (Choose up to 5 goals):

___Profit
___Revenue
___Marketing
___Customer Service
___Operations
___Culture
___IT

What is your overall vision statement for the goal you chose?:
To_____
_____.

Name a minimum of 3 Milestones to help you reach your goal with actionable steps under each milestone. Be sure to commit to a timeline:

Milestone #1:_____
action step: _____ timeline_____
action step: _____ timeline_____
action step: _____ timeline_____

Milestone #2:_____
action step: _____ timeline_____
action step: _____ timeline_____
action step: _____ timeline_____

Milestone #3:_____
action step: _____ timeline_____
action step: _____ timeline_____
action step: _____ timeline_____

BUSINESS GOAL WORKSHEET:

The 7 Areas of Business Development (Choose only up to 5 goals):

___Profit
___Revenue
___Marketing
___Customer Service
___Operations
___Culture
___IT

What is your overall vision statement for the goal you chose?:
To_____
_____.

Name a minimum of 3 Milestones to help you reach your goal with actionable steps under each milestone. Be sure to commit to a timeline:

Milestone #1:_____
action step: _____ timeline_____
action step: _____ timeline_____
action step: _____ timeline_____

Milestone #2:_____
action step: _____ timeline_____
action step: _____ timeline_____
action step: _____ timeline_____

Milestone #3:_____
action step: _____ timeline_____
action step: _____ timeline_____
action step: _____ timeline_____

BUSINESS GOAL WORKSHEET:

The 7 Areas of Business Development (Choose up to 5 goals):

__Profit
__Revenue
__Marketing
__Customer Service
__Operations
__Culture
__IT

What is your overall vision statement for the goal you chose?:
To_____
_____.

Name a minimum of 3 Milestones to help you reach your goal with actionable steps under each milestone. Be sure to commit to a timeline:

Milestone #1:_____
action step: _____ timeline_____
action step: _____ timeline_____
action step: _____ timeline_____

Milestone #2:_____
action step: _____ timeline_____
action step: _____ timeline_____
action step: _____ timeline_____

Milestone #3:_____
action step: _____ timeline_____
action step: _____ timeline_____
action step: _____ timeline_____

BUSINESS GOAL WORKSHEET:

The 7 Areas of Business Development (Choose up to 5 goals):

___Profit
___Revenue
___Marketing
___Customer Service
___Operations
___Culture
___IT

What is your overall vision statement for the goal you chose?:

To_____

_____.

Name a minimum of 3 Milestones to help you reach your goal with actionable steps under each milestone. Be sure to commit to a timeline:

Milestone #1:_____

action step: _____ timeline_____
action step: _____ timeline_____
action step: _____ timeline_____

Milestone #2:_____

action step: _____ timeline_____
action step: _____ timeline_____
action step: _____ timeline_____

Milestone #3:_____

action step: _____ timeline_____
action step: _____ timeline_____
action step: _____ timeline_____

GOAL-ALIGNMENT:
Accountability to Stay on Track!

After we create our vision, values, and goals—we can often hit hurdles and become disappointed. This can cause us to throw out the baby with the bath water, instead of staying open-minded to create the life we love!

To avoid abandoning your vision, values, and goals—ask yourself this accountability question to stay on point:

"Given my current circumstances, how might I still ALIGN to my vision, values and goals?"

JOURNAL: Think of one of your goals that has not unfolded as fast, or as well, as you would have hoped. Ask yourself the question above and journal about it.

By asking that very powerful question, *"How might I...?"*, you can raise your level of awareness regarding your choices, given your new circumstances.

JOURNAL:

Take this time to go back and look at your vision, values, and goals. Ask yourself these two questions:

1. Is this really what I want? Or is this something I think I should want or have?

2. If I really do want this, then:
   "How might I get it (given my circumstances)?"

PIVOT:
Be Fabulous!

PIVOT:
Gut Intelligence (GQ) to Notice Early Cues

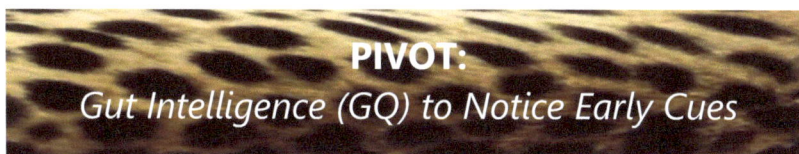

When you have increased Gut Intelligence (GQ), you can notice cues early on and pivot fast like the cheetah to create a life that is—fabulous! We all have had the experience where we had a ping in our gut that said, *"Pay attention—something's not going quite right and in alignment with what I want!"* When we have increased Gut Intelligence (GQ), we listen to that ping in our gut, make a wise assessment, and pivot fast with a decision that gets us back in alignment with what we want!

However, too often we don't trust our Gut Intelligence (GQ) and we:

- Go into DENIAL:
  We stick our head in the sand and pretend we don't know, because we don't want to deal with it.

- EMOTIONALLY REACT:
  We emotionally go into a "fight or flight" reaction—wanting to control the outcome because we're actually afraid we can't.

- Get into ANALYSIS-PARALYSIS:
  We get stuck in our head and try to figure everything out before we do or say anything (because deep down we are afraid we will miss something and fail!)

JOURNAL: Of the 3 reactions above, what is your tendency? When did you recently do this?

The good news is: Gut Intelligence (GQ) helps us pivot because it helps us to utilize the wisdom of our 3 brains:

- **Gut alerts us** to pay attention to cues at the tip of the iceberg

- **Heart aligns us** what we want in that moment of choice

- **Mind (head) assimilates the information** so we can see the possibilities at hand that best suit us

JOURNAL: Which of these three brains do you trust the most? Which do you trust the least? Why?

PIVOT:
3 Steps to Increased Gut Intelligence (GQ)

There are 3 Steps to Increased Gut Intelligence (GQ). They are:

Step #1: Own it! This means to own that gut-alert before you pivot.

Step #2: Ask it! This means to ask your intuition what is happening and what you need to do or say.

Step #3: Voice it! This means to voice your truth and let go of the outcome, trusting and allowing that *"this or something better is on its way!"*

JOURNAL: Which of the above three steps do you have the most difficulty doing? Why?

Let's define each one of these steps to help you understand how to increase your Gut Intelligence (GQ) and pivot!

Step 1: Own it!

When you own the gut alert, you get beyond the ego's fear that keeps you from increasing your Gut Intelligence (GQ) and listening to that Intuitive Inner Voice. The ego's mindset is one of fear, judgment, and control. The ego has two sides to it: Grandiosity and Self-Doubt.

Grandiosity side of the ego tends to:

- Pull up your bootstraps

- Think, "If it's meant to be, it's up to me!"

This is one way we dismiss our intuition.

The Self-doubt side of the ego tends to:

The other side of the ego does just the opposite. It believes:

- "I am not enough"
- "Life is not enough to support me"

To get beyond your ego's tendency, so you can increase your Gut Intelligence (GQ), simply notice which side of the ego you tend towards. Then, detach from that tendency.

JOURNAL: What is your ego's tendency: Grandiosity or Self-doubt?

Step #2: Ask it!

When we "Own it!" in step #1, we get out of the mindset of the ego, which is:

Fear, judgment, and control

When we "Ask it!" in step #2, we start a new mindset and way of being:

Open, trusting, and allowing Intuitive to guide us

This allows us to quiet our mind, let go of fear—and our ego—and engage our intuition instead.

Quieting the mind can best be done with: The S.T.O.P. Technique you previously learned on page 28.

JOURNAL: Where do you need to use the S.T.O.P. Technique right now?

Step #3: Voice it!

Now that you have used the S.T.O.P. Technique and understand how to use it to become intuitively aligned—it's time to "Voice it!".

The key to voicing it effectively is to invite someone into your authentic self. This means let them know your vision, values, and goals and how the decision you are making aligns to what is important to you.

Take the following quiz below to see how well you "Voice it!":

QUIZ: Voice it! (check in with yourself to see if you are being):

Rate yourself below to see how well you "Voice it!"

Rating: 1-Never, 2-Sometimes, 3-Average, 4-Mostly, 5-Always

___**Curious:** Do you "Voice it" in an open-minded and non-judgmental way?

___**Conscious:** Are you conscious of your ego's fear and any attachments you may have to the outcome before you "Voice it"?

___**Compassionate:** Do you "Voice it" in a way that is still considerate of the other person?

___**Courageous:** Are you able to "Voice it" in a vulnerable way that states what you want?

___**Connected:** Are you able to stay connected to this person & something bigger than this issue as you "Voice it"?

___**Collaborative:** Are you able to "Voice it" and still stay open to others suggestions?

___**Committed:** Are you committed to "Voice it" and stay intuitively aligned, regardless of your perceived outcome?

___Total Score

(If your score was 28 or above, mean you mostly voice it from your authentic self).

JOURNAL: What do you now know you need to do to improve so you can "Voice it!" authentically?

Use the worksheet below to help you Own it! Ask it! Voice it! –so you can pivot.

PIVOT: Journal Worksheet

Step 1: Own it!

When _____happened,

I felt scared_____

because_____

_____

_____.

Step 2: Ask it (Ask your intuitive that wants to shift you to your highest self)

How might I_____?

(Focus on what you want to create, not what you fear. Take several deep breaths in order to quiet your mind and listen within).

Step 3: Voice it

Be fearless: What is your intuition guiding you to do or say?

PIVOT:
The Heisenberg Theory

Often, we think judgmental thoughts in our head and believe we are not communicating them. As if no one knows what we are thinking! Did you know that communication is only 7 % words—the rest is body language and emotional energy? That means others can intuitively sense what you are thinking and feeling through your body language and emotional energy.

When we think thoughts like, "What a jerk!" –we are sending out that communication, even if it's not in words. "Voicing it" in such a passive way is not effective—and will not help us pivot. While someone can sense the judgment, this subtle communication does not allow for clear direction or resolution.

To illustrate the power of our thoughts, look at this thought model below:

Thoughts *create...*

Feelings *which create...*

Behavior *which create...*

Results!

When we are thinking a negative thought and have negative feelings; we will likely choose a negative behavior. Guess what result that leads to? A negative one!

Instead of choosing a negative thought, we can use the Heisenberg Theory and realize: *"That which we observe shifts!"*

When we think and wonder, "How might we get in alignment?"—we access our intuition to help us get out of fear and choose that just right conversation or decision to create what we want. When we allow our intuition to guide us, we become a powerful manifester.

To help you "Voice it", and use the Heisenberg Theory, use the 5 Step Intuitive Alignment Conversation on the next page. When you know you are going to have a hard conversation, practice this conversation in advance, so you can be prepared to "Voice it" in the most effective way.

JOURNAL: How might you have unconsciously created negative results in the past with your negative thoughts?

PIVOT:
5 Step Intuitive Alignment Conversation

The 5 Step Intuitive Alignment Conversation ensures we start a conversation in a positive way, with a general problem-solving question, instead of a blaming statement or complaint. Think of a situation where you need to "Voice it!" and use the process below:

5 Step Intuitive Alignment Conversation:

#1: Create a problem-solving question (How might we...?):
How might we _____?

#2: Listen: *(Seek to understand first and listen).*

#3: Feedback: *(Now feedback what you heard).*

#4: Speak your Truth & Voice it!

#5: Resolve:

Brainstorm ideas: (Don't argue, just share ideas. Write them down).

Now, choose your best ideas and create an action plan with the worksheet on the next page to ensure you move forward with resolution.

Action Plan:

	What	Who	When	Benchmark
1.				
2.				
3.				
4.				
5.				

Notes:

Now that you have learned how to:

- **AWAKEN** to your intuition—you can be *fearless*

- Create **GOAL-ALIGNMENT**—you can *focus* on your vision, values, and goals

- **PIVOT**—you can be *fabulous* and live a *fabulous* life!

You can be a woman who not only leads a fabulous life—you can also be a woman who shows up as a leader to others. When you stop trying to prove yourself and stop living by fear, judgment and control—you can, instead be more open, trusting and allowing intuition to guide you. As women, that is our leadership gift.

And when you live out your life in such a way, aligned to your inner authority, you show others how to live out their life in this way, at work and home. By your leadership example, others will understand what it takes to make decisions that align to their vision, values, and goals. This personal alignment will also help you align your decisions at work to the vision, values, and goals—so you can make a difference.

While people often think leadership means managing others, women leaders—who have taken this course—understand that leadership is actually an inside-out job. It begins with you being your fearless, focused, and fabulous self!

So, go ahead—love your life! Stay awaken, align your goals to what you love—and pivot fast when things aren't aligned. When you make this your habit—you will be like the cheetah!

By now, you have learned how to be fearless, focused & fabulous by awakening to your intuition, aligning your decisions to your goals, and pivoting when things are not as you desire. However, it's important to continue to listen to those pings in your gut and to notice those cues early on so you know when it's time to pivot!

That is why we have a Journal Section for you to help you continue to embody the spirit of the cheetah. Use the following journal pages to:

- Go back and review skills and journal on them

- Journal on current situations to clear the fear—and become your fearless, focused & fabulous self again

- Journal on that ping in your gut and what it might be trying to tell you

- Journal on your desires to get clearer about what you want

- Journal on your stress and anything on your mind!

Remember, the spirit of the cheetah helps us to contemplate before taking right action, so we can align our decisions to our vision, values, and goals! Journaling helps us do that—so we can increase our Gut Intelligence (GQ) and live our most fabulous life!

Did you know that what you focus on expands? And, what you think about you bring about! So, use journaling to become fearless, focused & to create the fabulous life you deserve!

JOURNAL:

JOURNAL:

JOURNAL:

JOURNAL:

JOURNAL:

JOURNAL:

JOURNAL:

JOURNAL:

JOURNAL:

JOURNAL:

JOURNAL:

JOURNAL:

JOURNAL:

JOURNAL:

JOURNAL:

JOURNAL:

JOURNAL:

JOURNAL:

JOURNAL:

Join
The Cheetah School for Women Leaders

Now, that you have learned how being like the cheetah can help you become more fearless, focused & fabulous...you likely want to learn more and continue your leadership growth!

That's why we created the online Cheetah School for Women Leaders. It's an online platform that brings the information from this book, plus other content, to video format. It also is an online platform that allows you to connect with other women business leaders, through our discussion board, available after each video lesson.

Because you have purchased this book already, use the following code to receive $50. off the Cheetah School Bundle Package: **IBoughtTheWomensLeadershipHandbook2021**

Redeem your coupon at The ALIGN Academy, where you will find the Cheetah School Bundle Package:
www.TheAlignAcademy.com

I hope to continue to work with you on your journey to become the fearless, focused & fabulous version of you—just like the cheetah!

Many Blessings-

Susan K. Wehrley

You can learn more about Susan's 10 other books at:
https://bizremedies.com/books/

www.ingramcontent.com/pod-product-compliance
Lightning Source LLC
Chambersburg PA
CBHW041716200326
41519CB00005B/265